What **80s**
Pop Culture
Teaches Us About
Today's Workplace

Mix Tape #1

Chris Clews

Illustrations by Jim Zielinski

For information about this title, contact the publisher:
Farmer Ted Publishing
farmertedpublishing@gmail.com

Published 2018 by Farmer Ted Publishing

19 18 17 1 2 3 4
ISBN
Paperback 978-1-7323351-2-7
eBook 978-1-7323351-3-4

Library of Congress Control Number: 2019931277

A portion of the proceeds from the sale of this book will benefit the animal welfare organization SPCA International.

"LIFE MOVES PRETTY FAST. IF YOU DON'T STOP TO LOOK AROUND ONCE IN A WHILE, YOU COULD MISS IT."
— Ferris Bueller

Dedication

This book is dedicated to my best friend, Dex, who passed in 2008 and had the greatest smile the world has ever known; John Hughes, who shaped and formed my teenage years and is the reason I will always wax nostalgic for the 80s; Ferris Bueller for always reminding me to embrace every day; the 80s boardwalk arcades that took all of my quarters during my summer quest to solve *Dragon's Lair* and taught me to never give up; my amazing family and incredible friends for their unwavering support; and to everyone out there who dreams big. Dream bigger. And then make it your reality.

Table of Contents

Preface

"Dear Mr. Vernon: We accept the fact that we had to sacrifice a whole Saturday in detention for whatever it is we did wrong. But we think you're crazy for making us write an essay telling you who we think we are. You see us as you want to see us: in the simplest terms, in the most convenient definitions. But what we found out is that each one of us is a brain, and an athlete, a basket case, a princess, and a criminal. Does that answer your question? Sincerely yours, The Breakfast Club."

CHAPTER 1
Ferris Bueller

"LIFE MOVES PRETTY FAST. IF YOU DON'T STOP TO LOOK AROUND ONCE IN A WHILE YOU COULD MISS IT."
- Ferris Bueller, Ferris Bueller's Day Off

I T WAS JUNE of 1986. Mr. Mister, Journey, George Michael, and Billy Ocean were dominating the Top 40 music charts. Top Gun and The Karate Kid Part 2 with Ralph Macchio were at the top of the movie box office. And The New York Times bestseller list harkened the arrival of a novel that would come to spawn a mega multi-media franchise: The Bourne Supremacy.

But the biggest impact of 80s pop culture would be felt on June 11th, 1986, when *Ferris Bueller's Day Off* debuted in theaters. John Hughes (get used to reading that name), who wrote and directed it had a knack for nailing the complexities of high school and what it took to navigate the hallways of our youth. The premise was simple: The class clown is determined to take the day off from school with his girlfriend and best friend Cameron, and in the process, he teaches the ultra-anxious Cameron how to live in the moment. As Ferris puts it, "If anybody needs a day off, it's Cameron. He's got a lotta things to sort out before he graduates. He can't be wound up this tight and go to college. His roommate will kill him."

Ferris, played brilliantly by Matthew Broderick, begins his day by convincing his parents that he is too sick to go to school. "They bought it. Incredible! One of the worst performances of my career, and they never doubted it for a second," he says gleefully. As he looks out of his window at the perfectly blue sky, Ferris continues, "How could I possibly be expected to handle school on a day like this?"

Sound familiar? You know you've done it as well. The difference is that Ferris got away with it—nine times, in fact. Of course, while Principal Rooney is pulling up Ferris' attendance records, the teen hacks in and changes his total absences from nine to two, prompting him to then say, "I asked for a car, I got a computer. How's that for being born under a bad sign?"

After both of his parents and the school are informed of his "illness," Ferris provides us with some details of his pre-planned day off via monologue. It is at this point that he gives a pearl of wisdom that is the basis for this chapter:

"Life moves pretty fast. If you don't stop to look around once in a while you could miss it".

I always felt like that was my mantra, and I've striven to embrace it as my philosophy for life. The problem was, for a long time, I didn't actually embrace it at all. The day I realized it, the truth hit me hard, and it has stuck with me ever since. I was working at an interactive ad agency in 1999. Yes, interactive advertising did actually exist back then. I hadn't seen my mom in quite a while, which was entirely my fault; a matter of that pesky work-life balance thing. She was flying in from out of state to spend the weekend with me. She was arriving on Friday, so we planned to meet for dinner at 7:00 that evening. Unfortunately, I was so caught up in a work project that I had to push dinner to 7:30. This turned into 8:30 and then 9:30.

When 9:30 came, I was still in my office. All the while, my mom was waiting patiently at the restaurant. We ended up getting room service at her hotel at around 10:00, three whole hours after our reservation. I left my mom waiting, and for what exactly? Work on a website project for a company that no longer existed just two years later. It wasn't an emergency deadline either. The website wasn't scheduled to be launched for two more weeks.

This painful episode—missing out on rare quality time with my mom—marks the moment when I decided to wholly embrace Ferris' philosophy. And though I haven't been perfect, those three hours are a constant and sometimes painful reminder of the importance of work–life balance.

So, what did the sage Ferris Bueller teach us about today's workplace and work–life balance with these nineteen words?

EMBRACE LIFE IN THE MOMENT

Embrace it. Take a day off work not because of a planned vacation or because you have a life event that needs attention. Take a day off to do something you've never done before. Do something fun. Do something crazy. Do something fun and crazy.

Ferris managed to sing in a parade; impersonate Abe Froman, "the Sausage King of Chicago" to sneak his friends into an elite restaurant; and convince Cameron to let the trio borrow his dad's 1961 Ferrari 250GT California as their transportation for their day off.

Fun Fact:

THE FICTIONAL FANCY RESTAURANT THAT FERRIS AND FRIENDS CON THEIR WAY TO A TABLE IN IS NAMED "CHEZ QUIS," A REFERENCE TO THE REAL WORLD PIZZA CHAIN, "SHAKEY'S."

After Cameron says, "My father spent three years restoring this car. It is his love. It is his passion," Ferris responds glibly, "It is his fault he didn't lock the garage."

I'm not suggesting that you spend your day the way Ferris did. It is a movie, after all. But spend it in a way that you can honestly say, "I stopped to look around, and I didn't miss it." And if you have a coworker or friend like Cameron; someone who is in a rut or has trouble with their own work–life balance, ask them to accompany you. They may try to resist at first, just like Cameron did with Ferris, but they might need it even more than you do, and when we do something to help a friend, we help ourselves in the process.

LIFE MOVES FAST

Life does move pretty fast. It sounds cliché, but college graduation feels like yesterday to me. Well, it wasn't. At the time of this writing, I just had my 25-year college reunion. So, yeah... not yesterday. Super-duper fast.

DON'T MISS WHAT MATTERS

Don't miss the events that matter with the people who matter. Those are the moments that matter most. A little of my Dr. Seuss for you there.

During the holidays especially, we all feel as if work–life balance is just out of reach. This is understandable. The end-of-year work demands are real and are a priority for all of us. Success in business and in life requires focus, determination, and hard work. Just do yourself a favor and don't wait for your "three-hour moment" before you decide to embrace those nineteen words.

And when you do decide to take that day off, remember what Ferris said when he was asked, "What are we going to do?"

Ferris replied, "The question isn't 'What are we going to do?' The question is 'What aren't we going to do?'"

CHAPTER 2

The Goonies

"GOONIES NEVER SAY DIE!"
- Mikey, *The Goonies*

I T WAS JUNE of 1985. Tears for Fears, Wham, Katrina & the Waves -- you can thank me later for having "Walking on Sunshine" stuck in your head for the rest of the week-- and Duran Duran were dominating the Top 40 music charts. People relaxing on the beach during their summer break were reading *The Vampire Lestat*, *Less Than Zero*, and all things Danielle Steele. *Beverly Hills Cop* and *Fletch* were at the top of the movie box office, along with the latest entry from the 80s power production team of Steven Spielberg and Richard Donner: *The Goonies*.

For those unfamiliar with the "Truffle Shuffle," The Goonies is an adventure comedy about a group of kids: asthmatic Mikey, played by a young Sean Astin; his big brother Brand, his friends Mouth, Chunk, and Data, and cheerleader Andy, and her friend Stef, all whose homes are set to be demolished by a developer. While devising a plan to save their neighborhood, they discover an old pirate map that sets them on a quest for hidden treasure left behind by the legendary pirate One-Eyed Willy. It's a classic 80s adventure in the realm of other greats in that genre, like *Time Bandits* and *The Explorers*; all from a time when "family" movies weren't just for kids.

Fun Fact:

SEAN ASTIN RECENTLY PLAYED BOB "THE BRAIN" NEWBY IN THE VERY 80S MOVIE-INSPIRED STRANGER THINGS SEASON 2.

"DOWN HERE, IT'S OUR TIME. IT'S OUR TIME DOWN HERE."
— Mikey

Throughout the movie, our merry and awkward band of Goonies face a multitude of challenges, including bullies, the destruction of their neighborhood, a family of ruthless bandits, a difficult-to-decipher treasure map, underground tunnels filled with skeletons, rats, and traps that split up the group; mental and physical exhaustion, disappearing floors, and even floods. And though there are moments when individual Goonies consider giving up, they stick together and lean on the unique strengths that each brings to the group. Together, they overcome the formidable set of obstacles and persevere. It is their time.

So, what did our lovable group of Goonies teach us about today's workplace?

NEVER GIVE UP

When Mikey stood up in front of the group and said, "Goonies never say die," it was at a moment when the others felt that the quest had become too difficult and the challenges too many to overcome. They were ready to give up en masse and accept their fates and failure as if they were predestined. At one point or another in our careers, most of us have felt overwhelmed, outmatched, or outmaneuvered. We've been on project teams whose members felt as though they have exhausted every possible avenue to success and that maybe that particular task was an exercise in futility; a bridge too far. This is also typically when the greatest feats are accomplished, and breakthroughs are just within reach. It is at these moments that the "Mikey" in you needs to kick into high gear. Take out your treasure map, lay it out in front of everyone, and look at it from a different angle. Find the path. It's there. Never give up. Never let the team give up. Never say die.

INCLUSION AND EMPATHY

As we established earlier, our group of lovable Goonies is quite the ragtag bunch. In some way, shape, or form, they are all outcasts who have spent their younger years running away from bullies or, worse yet, running away from who they really are. But at their core, they are all really good kids with big, accepting hearts and a desire to do the most good for the most people.

At one point, Chunk—of Truffle Shuffle fame—finds himself separated from the group and ends up captured by the Fratellis, a family of nefarious treasure-hunting bandits. They chain Chunk up in the basement of an abandoned restaurant. Noticing that someone else is chained up in the same room, Chunk begins making small talk and offers him a piece of his Baby Ruth candy bar. Unfortunately, he drops the candy bar just out of reach of his hulking cellmate, which infuriates the cellmate to the point where he screams and breaks out of his chains.

It is here that we meet Sloth, the outcast brother of our family of bandits, who has spent his life unloved and locked in the basement due to his physical appearance. He has missing teeth, one eye positioned substantially lower on his face than the other, different-sized ears that wiggle on their own, a severely crooked nose, a cone-shaped head with a small tuft of hair on top, and an odor that Chunk eloquently points out when he says, "Man, you smell like phys ed." Sloth would have a little trouble fitting in with most crowds, but not with the Goonies and not with Chunk who accepts him for who he is. Chunk looks past all the things on the outside, which so many would have used to judge Sloth. In return, he learns that the largest thing Sloth possesses is his heart, and his most prominent personality trait is his loyalty, which he puts on display when he is willing to put himself in harm's way to save the lives of the entire group of Goonies.

And this is where we learn our lesson. Our teams and our companies are stronger when we embrace everyone regardless of their cone-shaped heads, odd-looking ears that wiggle, or the fact that they may just "smell like phys ed."

It is often those we take for granted, isolate for ridiculous reasons, or overlook because of our own insecurities that have the answers to our questions, the solutions to the problems, and the inner strength to see things through to the end. Cliques are for high school, not for the workplace. Embrace everyone and we all succeed.

Now, if you are in a Goonies type of mood after reading this, walk into your office tomorrow and yell, "Hey, you guys!" I've done it, and it is exhilarating.

CHAPTER 3

Say Anything
and Lloyd Dobler

"I GAVE HER MY HEART AND SHE GAVE ME A PEN."
- Lloyd Dobler, *Say Anything*

IT WAS APRIL of 1989. I was a few months away from completing my freshman year at Elon College; now Elon University. The music charts were dominated by an eclectic group of acts including Poison, Bobby Brown, Samantha Fox, and Kenny G. The 80s really did have something for everyone. *Rainman, Twins,* and *Bill and Ted's Excellent Adventure* were cruising along in the box office. *Baywatch, The Simpsons, Seinfeld,* and *Family Matters*; all shows packed with memorable characters -- I think David

Hasselhoff is still selling out arenas in Germany-- each had their debut season.

Say Anything, directed by Cameron Crowe and starring John Cusack and Ione Skye, hit theaters on April 14th, 1989. Cusack played Lloyd Dobler, a senior in high school and aspiring kickboxer who refers to kickboxing as "the sport of the future." He crushes incredibly hard on Skye's character, Diane Court, who is the school valedictorian and is on a completely different life track from Lloyd.

While he has no real plans for his future beyond "being with your daughter; I'm good at it," as he tells her dad at dinner, she is scheduled to take up a fellowship in England at the end of the summer.

So, clearly, there is absolutely no way that the two of them would end up together, right? Oh, ye of little romantic comedy faith.

"I AM LOOKING FOR A DARE TO BE GREAT MOMENT."
— Lloyd Dobler

In one of the most iconic scenes in movie history, our awkward but endearing protagonist decides to go beyond the chocolates and flowers to win Diane's heart. He parks his sweet blue metallic Malibu down the street from her house, gets out, and proceeds to hold a large boom box over his head with Peter Gabriel's "In Your Eyes" cranking through the neighborhood on full blast. If nothing else, do yourself a favor and Google "Lloyd Dobler and Peter Gabriel." It's ninety seconds of 80s genius. It is his dare-to-be-great moment. Although it doesn't have the immediate impact he hopes for, it does make him memorable in her eyes. See what I did there?

So, what did the love-struck kickboxer Lloyd Dobler teach us about today's workplace?

TAKE THE DARE

For most of us, our jobs and, ultimately, our careers are very important to us. They define a portion of who we are. A portion. Not the whole. They are typically things that we are passionate about and things we care about. They are places where we feel we fit in and where we can find the greatest success, however you define it.

However, as we build our careers and our success, we can find ourselves following the old adage of "that's how we've always done it." We find a system or a process, and we continue to follow it day after day, year after year. It delivers results, so why not? Fair point. But does that attitude give you a chance to be memorable? Does it get people — better yet, your competition— talking? Does it go viral in the modern sense? Can you put your stake in the ground and say, "Our team did that"? Probably not.

Lloyd didn't rely on the staples: chocolate and flowers. Nope. He took the dare and used the great Peter Gabriel, a boom box, and a little ingenuity to create something memorable; something that would most certainly have gone viral had it been done in the internet age rather than the days of the touch tone phone.

So take the dare. Find your Peter Gabriel, use your ingenuity, and be memorable.

GIVING IT YOUR ALL AND GETTING A PEN

When Lloyd says, "I gave her my heart, and she gave me a pen," he is with his friends and recounting his last conversation with Diane before she leaves for England. Sitting in his car with her, Lloyd tells her how he feels. He shows her why he is the one for her. He does everything right. He gives it his all, and she gives him a pen. "Write me," she says before opening the door and leaving the car.

We've all been there at some point in our careers. You've given the job everything you can, and you've succeeded. The project you led is having a huge impact on revenue, the process you created is making the company incredibly efficient, or you've found a way to position the business for a new market that is full of opportunity. You're doing a great job, and people are noticing. This is the moment when you just know that a promotion and a raise are inevitable.

But it doesn't happen. There's an email announcement to all employees highlighting your efforts and thanking you. This makes you feel good. After all, it's good to be recognized, but it is better to be rewarded. While you gave your "heart," they gave you a "pen."

So, where do you go from here? Well, Lloyd does end up with Diane. He realizes that the pen represented her heart. It was all she could give at that moment. She was leaving for England, and her father had made it clear that he did not want her to spend any more time with Lloyd. In her quest to stay in touch, she gave him the pen and asked him to write to her. Remember, this was before cell phones or email were readily available. The pen represented the best she could give at that moment to let him know that she did care. It was her "heart."

Sometimes, what we perceive to be a slight is actually the best that someone can do at that time. There could be very real reasons why your company couldn't give you the raise or promotion, but they know it makes sense to give you something. The best way to do this may have been just to communicate their appreciation to all of your peers, acknowledging you as a leader and someone whom everyone should strive to emulate.

Ultimately, you may just get that raise and promotion, but not at the same time that you give your "heart." And if the reality is that the "pen" ends up being nothing more than a pen, it may be time to move on and find a company that embraces their inner Lloyd Dobler.

After all, you don't want your friends to freestyle burn you at the Gas-n-Sip on a Saturday night like Lloyd's do after his heart and pen story: "Lloyd, Lloyd, all null and void. Got dissed in the Malibu, don't know what to do."

Fun Fact:

EAGLE-EYED ENTOURAGE FANS MIGHT NOTICE A YOUNG JEREMY PIVEN SITTING CURBSIDE AT THE GAS-N-SIP.]

"Null and void." Twenty-eight years later, it still makes me laugh.

CHAPTER 4

Clark Griswold and Christmas Vacation

CLARK GRISWOLD: "IT'S A ONE-YEAR MEMBERSHIP TO THE JELLY OF THE MONTH CLUB."

COUSIN EDDIE: "CLARK, THAT'S THE GIFT THAT KEEPS ON GIVING THE WHOLE YEAR."
— Christmas Vacation

I T WAS DECEMBER of 1989. New Kids on the Block, Bobby Brown, Roxette, and Milli Vanilli topped the billboard charts. Stephen King and Tom Clancy were the authors of choice for those wanting to escape reality, and TV delivered the premiere episodes of *The Simpsons* and *America's Funniest Home Videos* while saying goodbye to *The Smurfs*. Back to the Future Part 2, The Little Mermaid, and Steel Magnolias were dominating the box office. Despite all the love I have for movies, I've actually only seen one of those, and no, it wasn't Steel Magnolias. Taylor Swift and Jordin Sparks were just born. Yeah, that doesn't make me feel old. Not normal old. More like *Lord of the Rings*, Gandalf-old.

On December 1st, everything at the box office changed when *Christmas Vacation*, directed by John Hughes, hit theaters, beginning its run as one of the greatest Christmas movies of all time. It was the third in a series of National Lampoon movies that followed the Griswold family and its patriarch, Clark, as he bumbled his way through the delicate art of family life and raising children. Clark, played by Chevy Chase, loves Christmas as much as Ferris loves his day off, and he does everything he can to please his family: his wife Ellen, played by Beverly D'Angelo; daughter Audrey, played by Juliette Lewis; and son Rusty, played by Johnny Galecki of *The Big Bang Theory* fame.

Fun Fact:

AUDREY AND RUSTY WERE EACH PORTRAYED BY SOMEONE NEW IN EVERY FILM IN THE FRANCHISE. IN THE LATEST INSTALLMENT, 2015'S VACATION, GROWN-UP AUDREY AND RUSTY WERE PORTRAYED BY LESLIE MANN AND ED HELMS, RESPECTIVELY.

Right from the outset, Clark just wants his family to have the best Christmas ever. From chopping down their own

Christmas tree, to decorating the house with enough lights to attract extraterrestrial life, to agreeing to host both sides of the family for the week, and, finally, to putting a down payment on a family swimming pool with his yet to be received work bonus, it's clear that Clark is determined to have the very merriest of Christmases.

By no surprise (this is a National Lampoon movie, after all) creating a very Merry Christmas for all isn't quite as easy as Clark initially thinks it will be. If you followed the Griswold clan through *Vacation* and *European Vacation*, you know that even the most well-intentioned plans are destined to fall completely apart before the memorable resolutions.

"YOU SURPRISED TO SEE US, CLARK?"
— Cousin Eddie

"OH, EDDIE, IF I WOKE UP TOMORROW WITH MY HEAD SEWN TO THE CARPET, I WOULDN'T BE MORE SURPRISED THAN I AM RIGHT NOW."
— Clark

So, what did our goofy family man, Clark Griswold, teach us about today's workplace?

STAY THE COURSE

Before his epic holiday meltdown, which I highly recommend you source on YouTube, when his bonus isn't what he expects it to be, Clark successfully navigates an obstacle course of holiday mishaps that make the labors of Hercules look benign by comparison. Here's the short list in this comedy of errors: A Christmas tree that is just a wee bit too big for the room shatters several of the neighbors' windows. Said Christmas tree also catches fire. 50,000 lights strung across the house with care over the course of an entire day don't light up during a grand family presentation. An overcooked Turkey crunches like peanut brittle when eaten. A dog vs. squirrel showdown results in the destruction of several rooms in the house. Clark gets locked in the attic when the family leaves for an event and proceeds to fall through the ceiling. A live cat, wrapped up as a gift, is not happy upon its release. There's the obnoxious yuppie couple next door, half of which is played by none other than Seinfeld's Julia Louis-Dreyfus. And worst of all, the surprise arrival of Cousin Eddie and his family in their run-down RV, complete with an overflowing sewage tank that Eddie, dressed in a ratty bathrobe, empties directly into the street in front of the Griswold house.

Yes, good old Clark certainly has a time of it, and it seems as though the universe has decided that his goal of creating a very Merry Christmas for his extended family is not to be. We've all been there at our places of business. We start with a goal that, on the surface, seems pretty easy to achieve, but along the way, we experience unusual surprises that keep taking us off course. Uncertainty creeps into what should have been a pretty straightforward exercise. Clark has his share of surprises as well, but through it all, he stays the course and keeps focused on his goal.

Ultimately, Clark succeeds. You can too. Stay the course. Embrace the unexpected hurdles along the way. Adapt as needed, but don't give up, and you'll reach your goal. It may just come in a slightly different package than you anticipated.

KNOW YOUR AUDIENCE

When Clark does have his epic meltdown after receiving the "one-year membership to the Jelly of the Month Club" as his annual work bonus, rather than the expected monetary sum that he had already spent on a swimming pool, he mentions that he would like a very unusual gift.

In front of his entire extended family, he states, "If any of you are looking for last-minute gift ideas for me, I have one. I'd like Frank Shirley, my boss, right here tonight. I want him brought from his happy holiday slumber over there on Melody Lane with all of the other rich people, and I want him brought right here with a big ribbon on his head . . ."

Cousin Eddie takes Clark's little rant literally and proceeds to drive to Melody Lane, kidnap Mr. Shirley, and deliver him to the Griswold residence in his pajamas. Needless to say, this was not really what Clark expected when he lost his ever-loving mind, but not every consequence is intended, especially when you are communicating with a diverse group of people. Eddie heard what he heard, and he acted on it. He wasn't blessed with the ability to analyze situations. He just wanted to solve Clark's problem and make him feel better. He didn't think about the fact that kidnapping was a felony and that the SWAT team would show up at the Griswolds' front door. Herein lies our lesson.

I work in marketing. My job involves communicating to large audiences, and though they tend to be targeted for a specific message, as individuals, they are very different. They think differently. They have different hobbies and interests. They live in different states and countries. They are unique individuals, and this is awesome. But it also means that they could potentially process words, statements, messages, and imagery differently. Whether it is the overall meaning, the time it takes to "get it," or the emotion it invokes, you have to be prepared for a variety of responses to your message: some good, some bad, some unexpected, and some... different. Be prepared, and expect the unexpected. Every message you deliver will return some surprises. Embrace them. Learn from them. And use them to make your next message even better.

It's a great big world out there with a great big group of diverse people just waiting to hear what you have to say. Tell them all about your product or service and your organization or business, and be prepared for their responses. They may surprise you, and you'll most certainly learn something in the process, but the more you know your audience, the more prepared you'll be for how they react to your message. And if you've done your due diligence, they should react exactly as you would like them to.

One more thing on Cousin Eddie: Every workplace has one. Some have multiple, and even though he may make you want to pull your hair out from time to time, he probably has the biggest heart of anyone. You may not always be able to depend on him to deliver his best work on every single project, but you can bet that you can always count on his friendship and loyalty. And while a project is for the short term, loyal friends are forever.

And if you do get a "Jelly of the Month Club" membership as a gift—"It's the gift that keeps on giving the whole year," as Cousin Eddie says—just be grateful it isn't a "Fruitcake of the Month Club." That, I think we can all agree, is definitely not the gift that keeps on giving the whole year.

Finally, if you've learned nothing else, don't spend your bonus before you have it!

CHAPTER 5
Beverly Hills Cop and Axel Foley

"I DON'T KNOW WHAT YOU TEACH THESE FELLOWS, BUT THEY'RE NOT JUST REGULAR COPS. THEY'RE SUPER COPS. AND THE ONLY THING MISSING ON THESE GUYS ARE CAPES."

— Axel Foley, *Beverly Hills Cop*

I T WAS DECEMBER of 1984. Orwell's vision of the future was a little premature. I was in my freshman year of high school. I'm pretty sure that I had braces and headgear, Farmer Ted style. Once again, as the decade was wont to provide, the music charts were dominated by an outrageous but talented mix of musicians, including the mainstay duo of Hall and Oates, 50s throwbacks The Honeydrippers, some Irish rock band named U2, and the modern-day barbershop quartet New Edition. Go ahead. I know you remember: "Cool it now, you got to cool it now . . ." Sing it loud and proud. Chuck Norris was killing at the box office with *Missing in Action*, Robert Englund as Freddie Krueger was doing some killing of his own with *A Nightmare on Elm Street*, and Arnold Schwarzenegger was introducing the phrase "I'll be back" into the American lexicon with *The Terminator*. Television was having a modern-day renaissance, with *Cheers, Newhart, The A-Team*, and *The Cosby Show*. And a show called *The Duck Factory*, which lasted all of three months, introduced us to the mad genius that is Jim Carrey. It was his first leading role, and I think we can all agree that he did okay after that debut.

Beverly Hills Cop, an action comedy starring Eddie Murphy, hit theaters on December 5th, 1984 and immediately shot straight to number one. Murphy, whose comedy star was shining very brightly in the early 80s, played the street-smart and rebellious Detroit detective Axel Foley. His search for his childhood friend Mikey's killer takes him to Beverly Hills under the pretense of a "vacation" after his superior officer, Inspector Todd, played by Gilbert R. Hill, denies Axel the option to pursue the case. Do yourself a favor, and find Hill's scenes online. He owns each one, even those with Eddie Murphy. Seriously, he's spectacular. And he was a real-life police officer in Detroit when he was discovered. You can't get more authentic than that.

Fun Fact:

BEVERLY HILLS COP IS FULL OF GREAT ACTORS IN SMALL PARTS, INCLUDING DAMON WAYANS IN HIS FIRST FILM APPEARANCE, AND JOHNATHAN BANKS AS ZACK, THE MAN WHO KILLED MIKEY. BANKS IS BEST KNOWN TODAY FOR PLAYING MIKE EHRMANTRAUT IN BREAKING BAD AND BETTER CALL SAUL.

When Axel arrives in Beverly Hills, he confronts Victor Maitland, the man he believes is behind the killing of his friend, and is promptly arrested for disturbing the peace and carrying a concealed weapon after being thrown through a glass window by Maitland's bodyguards. The arresting officers, Sergeant John Taggart, played by John Ashton; and Detective Billy Rosewood, played by Judge Reinhold, take him to their lieutenant, who has been made aware that Axel is in town for an unsanctioned investigation against the wishes of Detroit PD. He is warned to give up his search and enjoy California as a tourist or face the consequences, i.e., arrest in Beverly Hills and the loss of his job in Detroit. Of course, as I am sure you'd guess, he doesn't listen.

Taggart and Rosewood become Axel's allies through the chaos that ensues, including gunfights, car chases, kidnappings, awkward arrests, multiple impersonations, Axel having his name butchered numerous times by the inimitable character actor Bronson Pinchot, and one perfectly ripe banana in a tailpipe.

After the smoke clears, Axel Foley does of course get his man. Despite a myriad resources, money, technology, and shiny new toys, the Beverly Hills PD is no match for the guts, instinct, intelligence, and determination of Detective Foley, who, in the process of solving his friend's murder, also breaks up a massive drug ring that the Beverly Hills PD has been trying to disrupt for years.

So, what did our hard-nosed but charming detective, Axel Foley, teach us about today's workplace?

PROTECT YOUR TEAM, EVEN IF YOU HAVE TO STRETCH THE TRUTH A LITTLE

When Axel said of Taggart and Rosewood, "I don't know what you teach these fellows, but they're not just regular cops. They're super cops. And the only thing missing on these guys are capes," he and his BHPD partners found themselves in a bit of a bind. Axel had convinced Taggart and Rosewood to visit an adult establishment during work hours on a hunch that someone they were pursuing might be there. Things didn't go as planned, to say the least. While the trio was sitting at their table, which just happened to be directly in front of the main stage, an armed robbery was attempted. It was attempted but not committed because it was broken up by our three protagonists.

While this would normally be grounds for an award, it actually became grounds for dismissal from their jobs when they returned to the office. As the de facto leader of the group, Axel spun a story to their lieutenant, positioning Taggart and Rosewood as heroes, even throwing himself under the bus by claiming that they were simply tailing Axel, as ordered, to make sure he didn't continue doing police work in Beverly Hills.

Axel went on to say that the only reason they came inside was because they witnessed "two suspicious-looking gentlemen with bulges in their jackets walking into the club." Even though it was actually Axel who first spotted the potential armed robbers and, ultimately, got the jump on them, he gave his team members all of the credit to protect them when they were in a very dicey situation.

Straight-laced Taggart and Rosewood came clean about what happened, prompting Axel to say, right in front of the lieutenant, "The super cop story was working. Okay? It was working, and you guys just messed it up. Okay? I'm trying to figure you guys out, but I haven't yet. It's cool. You [messed] up a perfectly good lie, and... it's alright." Even in defeat prompted by their own actions, he continued to let his team know that he would protect them in the future at any cost, including admitting to his own lie in front of their boss. And he did it with a little humor. Humor always wins the day.

Protect and defend your team at any cost, especially when all of you are in the line of fire. They won't forget it.. And if you have a good boss, you might be surprised by his or her reaction.

YOUR BEST RESOURCE IS YOU

"THIS IS THE CLEANEST AND NICEST POLICE CAR I HAVE EVER BEEN IN. THIS IS NICER THAN MY APARTMENT."
— Axel Foley

When Axel arrived in Beverly Hills, he had his gun and his badge, but both were taken away when he was arrested for disturbing the peace after being thrown through a window. To this, he replied, "Disturbing the peace? I got thrown out of a window. What's the charge for getting pushed out of a moving car, huh? Jaywalking?"

So, here is Detective Axel Foley. No gun. No badge. No tools at all. Just the clothes on his back. And here is the Beverly Hills PD with its state-of-the-art everything; computers, GPS, technology galore, more cops than the city of Detroit had people. They had enough guns and ammo for their own military, mahogany-lined offices, and really clean and nice police cars that were, as Axel noted, "nicer than my apartment." Axel wasn't granted access to any of it. Sean Connery wouldn't even have been able to accuse him of bringing a knife to a gunfight. Yeah, that was Axel. But Axel was motivated and determined to solve Mikey's murder and, in the process, bring down the head of and organized crime ring; a guy hiding in plain sight just under the nose of the very well-resourced BHPD.

So, how would Axel, find a way to outmaneuver his well-resourced competitor? He didn't use his situation as an excuse. After losing his gun and his badge, it would have been easy to give up and admit defeat. After all, the BHPD was loaded with the finest tools and resources. If they couldn't do it, what chance did he have?

Instead of wallowing, complaining, or giving up, Axel used the best tools he had available: instinct, guts, intelligence, ingenuity, intuition, and pure grit; a hell of an internal toolbox. It contained impersonations to get into places he couldn't enter on his own, charisma to charm the right people and the wrong ones, salesmanship and confidence to convince the most experienced police officers to follow his lead, and perhaps the best example of doing more with less: one perfectly selected and perfectly placed banana in a tailpipe. He was absolutely determined to win, and he wasn't going to be intimidated by a well- connected and well-financed crime boss or a bigger, "badder," and better-financed competitor in the BHPD.

Sound familiar? Well, not the crime boss part, I hope, but the bigger, "badder," and better-financed competitor. We've all been there at some point. Maybe it was the final job interview for a position that you knew was right for you even if you might be the least experienced person to fill the role. Maybe it was the final pitch to a game-changing prospective client, and your small start-up was one of their final three options, but your two competitors were larger, more experienced, and had very impressive global client lists. Or maybe you finally decided to venture out on your own, start your own business, and set sail in your wooden rowboat as you prepare to do battle with the superyachts and destroyers.

Whatever the situation, you are your best resource. Sure, competing against someone who has unlimited resources and the very best tools at their disposal might put you at a disadvantage, but consider how much of that is up to the individual.

Remember that big, bad competitor was once just like you, outgunned and under-resourced. But they used their internal toolkit just like Axel and became the king or queen of the hill. Now, it's your turn. No excuses. Turn on your Detroit. Find your inner Axel Foley.

CHAPTER 6
Back To The Future

"DON'T WORRY. AS LONG AS YOU HIT THAT WIRE WITH THE CONNECTING HOOK AT PRECISELY EIGHTY-EIGHT MILES PER HOUR, THE INSTANT THE LIGHTNING STRIKES THE TOWER, EVERYTHING WILL BE FINE."
— Dr. Emmett Brown, *Back To The Future*

I T WAS JULY of 1985. I had a summer job washing dishes to make money to buy a super-sweet, two-cassette-deck boom box. I would be the envy of my town. Not really, but a kid can dream. The summer box office was heating up. One of the all-time great movies, *The Goonies* (please don't remake it, please don't remake it), was successfully taking kids and their parents to a make-believe underground world, while *Cocoon* was taking parents and their parents on a journey to a make-believe fountain of youth. Meanwhile, Clark Griswold was having trouble "getting left" during the second family trip in *European Vacation*, Clint Eastwood was playing a mysterious cowboy (shocking, I know) in *Pale Rider*, and the brat pack was living up to its name in *St. Elmo's Fire*.

The billboard music charts continued their love for the combination of one-hit wonders and future Rock-n-Roll Hall of Fame inductees, including Harold Faltermeyer's theme song from *Beverly Hills Cop*, The Fine Young Cannibals, Kool and the Gang, and Tears for Fears. Television was having a great year, with the premieres of *Growing Pains, Moonlighting, The Golden Girls*, and *227*. Perhaps the greatest achievement in television in 1985, in my humble opinion, also occurred in July, on July 1st, to be exact; it was the launch of Nick at Nite. And why was that such a great achievement? Well, it paved the way for TV Land, a station dedicated to the great shows of yesteryear. Today, that means that from 11 p.m. to 1 a.m. every night, I get to watch four episodes of Friends, and that, my friends, is wondrous and joyful. It means that Phoebe, Joey, Rachel, Ross, Monica, Chandler, and, my favorite, Janice, will entertain this night owl for years to come.

Back to the Future, starring Michael J. Fox and directed by Robert Zemeckis, hit theaters on July 3rd of 1985. Someone named Steven Spielberg was also an executive producer, but no one really knew who he was or ever heard from him again. Marty McFly, played by Fox, is a 17-year-old high school student who is sent plummeting 30 years into the past via the coolest car of the 80s, the DeLorean. This baby is a time-traveling DeLorean thanks to a plutonium-powered invention called a flux capacitor created by our lesson leader for this chapter, Dr. Emmett Brown. During his time travels, Marty unwittingly gets in the way of his high school-aged parents meeting and falling in love. He realizes that the only way to fix this and make sure that he actually exists in the future is to find his friend Doc Brown in 1955, prove that he is actually from the future, get Doc's help to bring the teenage versions of his parents back together, and then send him... back to the future!

Fun Fact:

BESIDES PENNING AND PERFORMING "THE POWER OF LOVE" AND "BACK IN TIME," HUEY LEWIS OF HUEY LEWIS AND THE NEWS PLAYED AN UNCREDITED HIGH SCHOOL BAND AUDITION JUDGE.

As you can imagine, things don't go quite as simply as expected. OK, if that sounded simple to you, I'd like to go back in time and cheat off of you in high school algebra. Seriously, when they put the numbers with the letters? 2x+y=10? That just hurt my head writing it. But I digress. With Doc Brown on board Marty explains what they need to get him back to 1985. When Marty reveals that they will need 1.21 gigawatts (pronounced "jigawatts" throughout the movie) of power and plutonium to make it happen, Doc replies with, "I'm sure that in 1985, plutonium is available in every corner drug store, but in 1955, it's a little hard to come by. Marty, I'm sorry, but I'm afraid you are stuck here."

Doc continues to say, "The only power source capable of generating 1.21 gigawatts of electricity is a bolt of lightning." Conveniently, Marty was carrying a flyer that he received in own his time that states exactly when the clock tower in the town square is going to be hit by lightning. At this point, Doc makes it clear to Marty that he must avoid any situations that could impact the future, and he tells him that he cannot leave the residence until they find a way to send him home with that lightning strike. Marty explains that he has already run into his mom and dad, to which Doc Brown replies with his now-classic saying, "Great Scott!" and the race to set things right and send Marty back to the future begins.

Fun Fact:

WITHOUT GETTING TOO DEEP INTO THE PHYSICS, 1.21 GIGAWATTS ACTUALLY IS A TREMENDOUS AMOUNT OF POWER, AND A WELL-TIMED BOLT OF LIGHTNING MIGHT ACTUALLY BE ONE OF THE MORE REALISTIC SOURCES FOR THAT AMOUNT OF ENERGY IN THAT SHORT OF A MOMENT.

Although Marty is our main protagonist, it is actually Doc Brown who provides us with the knowledge that we need to survive and thrive in the most impossible of situations.

So what did the eccentric, frazzled, genius Doctor Emmett Brown teach us about today's workplace?

ANSWER EVERY CHALLENGE

When Doc Brown said, "Don't worry. As long as you hit that wire with the connecting hook at precisely eighty-eight miles per hour, the instant the lightning strikes the tower... everything will be fine," it was an incredibly poor, albeit humorous, attempt to help Marty relax, as the moment to send him back to the future was rapidly approaching. It was the moment that would either return him to his life in 1985 or leave him stuck in 1955. Sure, seems simple enough. No pressure, McFly.

We've all been there when a work challenge seems insurmountable; dare I say "impossible"? Lots of moving parts, unreasonable timing, an untested resource, and you've got one opportunity to get it right. It is in these moments that many of us begin to feel an overwhelming sense of doom, and some of us begin to think about our exit plans. Don't go there. C'mon, if Patrick Dempsey can go from nerd extraordinaire in the 1987 classic romantic comedy *Can't Buy Me Love* to the dapper and handsome "Dr. McDreamy" on the television show *Grey's Anatomy*, well, then nothing is impossible.

Answer the challenge. If you are the process-oriented type, bite off pieces of the project and take it one step at a time. Don't overwhelm yourself with everything that has to happen all at once. Take it "Step by Step," just like New Kids On The Block taught you. You'll time the lightning strike perfectly.

Fun Fact:

THAT PARTICULAR NKOTB SONG WAS RELEASED IN 1990, BUT THE BOY BAND WAS FORMED IN THE LATE 80S, SO I THINK IT'S STILL VALID 80S POP CULTURE.

Alternatively, if you are like me and prefer the "I'll figure it out along the way" approach, then embrace the chaos, hop in the DeLorean, put the pedal to the metal, and use your Magnum P.I. "little voice inside" to guide you. It may not always get you to exactly eighty-eight mph, but if you stay on top of the project and make the necessary adjustments along the way, you should be able to hit somewhere between 85 and 89 mph, and it may surprise you just how good that really is. Worst-case scenario, you end up in 1983 or 1987, which isn't really that far off in the scheme of things. And besides, they were awesome years for pop culture, so there is always that.

BE A VISIONARY

"ROADS? WHERE WE'RE GOING, WE DON'T NEED ROADS."
— Dr. Emmett Brown

At the end of the movie, Doc Brown; Marty; and Marty's girl-friend, Jennifer are in the DeLorean heading to the year 2015 when Marty expresses concern about the small stretch of neighborhood street ahead of them. "Doc, you better back up. We don't have enough road to get up to eighty-eight."

Doc Brown replies, "Roads? Where we're going, we don't need roads."

By now, Doc had upgraded the DeLorean with technology from the future he had already visited, but when he first built the time machine, it was all about the unknown. He had a mission of discovery ahead of him, and he was determined to pursue it. It's this last part that is the most important: He believed in his vision. The greatest of our inventors and visionaries believe that there is something greater out there even if they don't necessarily know where their vision is going to take them or if what they believe is actually possible. However, just like our eccentric genius Doc Brown, they always speak with confidence about their vision, inspiring those around them to believe as well.

Most people follow someone else's vision, and that's okay, but how awesome would it be if that vision was yours? We all have that inside of us, the ability to see something that others don't. I don't mean in a *Sixth Sense*, "I see dead people" sort of way, although that would be super cool. Maybe. I mean, if they weren't scary ghosts. When your team believes in your vision, they will follow you, even if deep down, they also know that the journey is uncertain and none of you are really sure if you'll actually need roads where you are going or not. It doesn't matter. They believe because you believe, and this makes you a visionary.

None of us can go "Back in Time" as Huey Lewis sings, but we can chart a course for our future. Let's just hope it doesn't require a DeLorean, 1.21 gigawatts of power, and a flux capacitor to get there. Although, as Doc Brown says, "The way I see it, if you're gonna build a time machine into a car, you might as well do it with some style."

CHAPTER 7
E.T.

"BE GOOD."
– E.T.

I T WAS JUNE of 1982. I had just graduated from 6th grade. I was getting ready to go from the king of elementary school to the king of the dorks as I entered the much larger and more intimidating halls of middle school. Like a typical twelve-year-old boy, I was going through Clearasil faster than the girls in my class went through a can of non-ozone-friendly hairspray. With the school year ending, the production companies began releasing their "can't miss" summer movies. Harrison Ford, minus the whip and hat, starred in the futuristic *Blade Runner*. Sylvester Stallone took on my favorite of the Rocky villains, Clubber Lang, who delivered the classic prediction of simply "Pain" for the for the fight to come in *Rocky 3*. The pre-

JJ Abrams *Star Trek 2: The Wrath of Khan* was entertaining audiences with a super heavy dose of overacting. And at completely opposite ends of the intellectual spectrum were the raunchy college coming-of-age comedy *Porky's* and the poignant, artistic, beautifully shot eventual Oscar winner *Chariots of Fire.*

The billboard music charts were as mixed up as my sense of fashion at the time, given my proclivity for parachute pants and Members Only jackets. Great new-wave bands, including The Human League with "Don't You Want Me?" and Soft Cell with "Tainted Love," were surrounded by arena rockers like Asia; country icon Willie Nelson; one of the original female power rockers, Joan Jett; and the voice behind the *Ghostbusters* theme song, Ray Parker Jr. And let's not forget the music royalty duo, Paul McCartney and Stevie Wonder, who were dominating the number-one spot with "Ebony and Ivory."

Television viewers saw the premieres of two classic sitcoms: *Newhart* and *Cheers. Fame, Family Ties,* and the mercifully short-lived *Joanie Loves Chachi* premiered as well. We said goodbye to *In Search of...,* hosted by Leonard Nimoy; *WKRP in Cincinnati* (I still miss Les Nesman and Venus Flytrap); *Mork & Mindy,* and *Bosom Buddies,* the show that put Tom Hanks on the map.

Fun fact:

BOB NEWHART GUEST STARS ON THE BIG BANG THEORY AS PROFESSOR PROTON, SHELDON'S CHILDHOOD HERO. LEONARD NIMOY MADE A FEW APPEARANCES ON THE POPULAR SHOW AS WELL, BUT AS HIMSELF.

E.T. the Extra-Terrestrial, starring Henry Thomas and directed by Steven Spielberg, hit theaters on June 11th of 1982. It is the story of a friendly, empathic alien who gets stranded on Earth when his spaceship leaves without him. Luckily for him, he is discovered by a compassionate and loyal boy named Elliott, who does everything he can to protect E.T. from numerous factions of the federal government and local law enforcement.

While E.T. tries to make sense of his new surroundings, Elliott works hard to gain his trust, as both are in a race against time to help him find his way home. Along the way, they teach each other life lessons about compassion, loyalty, patience, when to fight and when to flee, trust, and love.

E.T. does the opposite of Eric Clapton by actually finding his way home (audiophiles will get that one), but not before he finds himself lying on the side of a riverbed pallid except for fading red light put off by glowing heart. I weep uncontrollably every time I see E.T. on the side of that riverbed. I didn't have that strong of an emotional reaction to a movie again until Wilson the volleyball floated away from Tom Hanks during the brutal storm at sea in *Castaway*. Yes, as Hanks yelled, "Wilson, I'm sorry!" Yes, I wept uncontrollably for an extra-terrestrial and a volleyball. And so did you.

So, what did the compassionate human boy Elliot and the gentle alien from billions of miles away, E.T., teach us about today's workplace?

FIND A CAUSE

As he prepares to leave Earth, E.T. gives Elliot's little sister Gertie, played by a very young Drew Barrymore, a simple instruction: "Be good." He is echoing Elliot's request for E.T. to behave himself while Elliot attended school and left E.T. home alone earlier in the film. "Be good" were the last words that we heard E.T. speak, and they summed up his personality and presence perfectly.

Fun fact:

HARRISON FORD, INDIANA JONES AND HAN SOLO HIMSELF, PLAYED THE PRINCIPAL IN A DELETED SCENE THAT ORIGINALLY WAS TO FOLLOW ELLIOT'S SCIENCE CLASS EXCITEMENT. YOU CAN CATCH HIM IN THE SPECIAL FEATURES OF THE DVD OR BLU-RAY RELEASES.

One of my favorite scenes is one of the subtler moments. When E.T. noticed a pot of dead flowers in Gertie's room, he looked at them, focused and made a little alien sound, and they immediately bloomed in full. Throughout the movie, E.T. does things that encapsulate his "be good" mantra, and he clearly has an empathic bond with any living being, including flowers. We can literally see his heart glowing in his chest. That's a close as a naked alien creature gets to wearing their heart on their sleeve.

I'm not sure any of us can glance at dead flowers and make them bloom. If you can, we are going to Vegas together. Anyone can, however, have an impact on someone or something that needs it and "be good." In the last decade, businesses have embraced cause marketing and social responsibility and have given their employees the workplace flexibility to do the same. Whether it is giving paid time off for volunteering, providing real resources to those in need, committing a percentage of profits to a cause, or supporting charitable organizations with the products they create or services they render, many corporations are making an investment in being good. E.T. would be proud.

If you work for a company that hasn't quite found its "be good" footing, take the initiative; propose something and find people who can help you make it happen. It takes just one person to create a make-a-difference philosophy within your company culture. Be that person.

Alternatively, if you are starting your own business, there are plenty of success stories out there of recently launched companies that started with an absolute mission to be good. They didn't wait for the revenues and growth to happen first. They tied their revenues and growth to being good from the very first dollar earned. TOMS, the footwear company, makes a one-to-one donation for every pair of shoes purchased. Warby Parker donates a pair of glasses to a nonprofit organization for every pair of glasses purchased. Yoobi donates the same number of school supplies purchased through the company to United States schools in need. These are just a few, and there are more coming every day.

You don't need to literally see your heart glow to know how good it feels to make a difference where one is desperately needed. Let you and your company's inner E.T. shine through. Be good.

GO HOME

"E.T. phone home." When E.T. stated his directive, it immediately stuck as one of the great and memorable movie lines, up there with Dirty Harry's "Go ahead; make my day" and Rocky's "Yo, Adrian." The difference was the meaning of those three words to the overall message and theme of the movie and, of course, what we can learn from them for our businesses. Rocky could be a cool movie to diagnose one day, but it might be a slight struggle to figure out what "Yo Adrian" could teach us about the workplace. I'll ponder that one.

Throughout the movie, E.T. had a singular mission: to go home. Think about what he had to overcome to accomplish this task. Stranded billions of miles away, government agencies using all their resources to capture him, a language he didn't speak, no way to communicate with his loved ones to let them know where he was, an unfamiliar geography, and not knowing with whom or where to place his trust. Of course, something very easy for E.T. was the decision to follow and consume a trail of Reese's Pieces left behind by Elliot to guide him into the house.

We can disagree on a lot of things, but anything that combines peanut butter and chocolate makes my heart light up just like

41

E.T.'s. Honestly, I look at people who don't like the combination of peanut butter and chocolate the same way I look at people who don't like dogs, slightly askew and with a furrowed brow. A little crazy? Maybe. But that is my unconditional love for all things peanut butter and chocolate.

Truthfully, E.T. had a heck of a trial to overcome to find his way home. The challenges were massive and intense, and there was a very real possibility that he would die trying. But that didn't stop him, and despite all these obstacles, he did make it home. Going home for us is much easier than it was for E.T., yet many of us consistently put our work before our loved ones. We keep promising ourselves that we will get there for the next holiday, birthday, or dinner. We keep meaning to plan that long weekend with friends back in our hometowns. For some, it is as simple as making it home for dinner with the family, but even this doesn't happen because "something came up at work at the last second." Some of these things absolutely need to be handled immediately. We all make sacrifices for the careers that we love. It's totally understandable and even admirable. But, unless you are a transplant surgeon or homicide detective, the majority of these "somethings" can wait. And if they can wait, then they should.

Unlike E.T., who had to find a way to signal his family from billions of miles away and then hitch a ride home on a spaceship, we have a variety of ways to "go home." For those of us whose families and loved ones live in a different location, we can purchase a plane ticket, hop in a car, or take a train, bus, or even an Uber. These days, even if you can't do that, you can use Skype, FaceTime, WhatsApp, or any variety of video chat applications. And for those who have families, partners, spouses, or dogs (cats too, I guess) waiting for them each evening, go home! Go now. They are worth it, and so are you. There will always be more "last-second work things," but we have only so much time to create the memories that really matter. And who knows? Maybe you'll get super lucky and dessert will be Reese's Pieces. If nothing else, this will make it all worthwhile.

CHAPTER 8
Stand By Me

"ALRIGHT, ALRIGHT. MICKEY'S A MOUSE, DONALD'S A DUCK, PLUTO'S A DOG. WHAT'S GOOFY?"
—Gordie, Stand By Me

IT WAS AUGUST of 1986. I was preparing for my junior year of high school by getting lines shaved into the hair on the side of my head and coloring them green for effect. Yeah, I did that. Mercy. With the end of summer rapidly approaching, the box office was still awash with blockbusters. In those days, movies stayed in theaters longer than a fortnight. In fact, some continued to sell tickets for months before eventually going the way of the VHS tape and the "coming soon" board with white plastic lettering in your local video store. *The Fly*, with Jeff Goldblum; the sci-fi horror classic *Aliens*; and the wax on, wax off return of Ralph Macchio and Pat Morita in *Karate Kid 2* were amassing massive sales of $3.00 movie tickets. It was also the year the world was introduced to Maverick, Goose, and Iceman in the American classic *Top Gun*.

The Top 40 in music was once again proving that the 80s most certainly had something for everyone. The classic sounds of Steve Winwood reverberating through "Higher Love"; the one-hit wonder Jermaine Stewart with his super-catchy ode to morals in "We Don't Have to Take Our Clothes Off"; Peter Cetera, who was to the Karate Kid trilogy what John Williams was to Star Wars, gave us his latest ballad, "The Glory of Love"; and the female alt pop band Bananarama had their smash hit "Venus." Even with all of these are battling their way to the tip of your tongue, I would be remiss not to recognize the most inventive of songs in 1986, one that launched a new sound that is often imitated but never duplicated. This was that year in which Run DMC and Aerosmith combined their massive forces for a rap/rock remake of "Walk this Way," a mind-blowing move for the time.

Television gave us the first attempt at a new network since 1967 with the launch of the Fox Television Network, which immediately hit it big with Al and Peggy Bundy in *Married with Children*. We also first met *ALF*, the lovable Alien Life Form with an attitude, who was pushing the FCC envelope. *L.A. Law* was drawing in huge ratings with its version of *Baywatch* in the courtroom; and one of my favorites, *Perfect Strangers* with Bronson Pinchot began. We also said goodbye to some all-time greats, with *Different Strokes* ("What'chu you talkin' 'bout, Willis?"), *The Love Boat* ("Love, exciting and new"), *Benson*, with the incredibly talented Robert Guillaume, and *The Fall Guy* with Lee Majors and Heather Thomas, the latter of whom might be best remembered for a popular poster adorning many a teenaged boy's room. I had one. Maybe two.

Fun Fact:

AL BUNDY ACTOR ED O'NEILL IS CURRENTLY JAY PRITCHETT IN MODERN FAMILY, DESTINED TO GO DOWN AS ANOTHER OF THE GREATEST SITCOMS OF ALL TIME.

Stand by Me, directed by Rob Reiner, hit theaters on August 8th of 1986. The coming-of-age comedy drama tells the story of four junior high school boys: Gordie, played by Wil Wheaton; Chris, played by River Phoenix; Vern, played by Jerry O'Connell; and Teddy, played by Corey Feldman. The friends venture out to find a missing neighborhood kid whose body is supposedly located somewhere near the railroad tracks. The story takes place in the fictional town of Castle Rock, Oregon over Labor Day weekend in 1959. The movie is narrated by Richard Dreyfuss as a grown-up version of Gordie, now a published writer recounting their journey after reading that Chris has been stabbed to death trying to break up a fight at a fast food restaurant.

Fun Fact:

STAND BY ME IS BASED ON A NOVELLA BY STEPHEN KING TITLED THE BODY, IT WAS INCLUDED IN HIS BOOK DIFFERENT SEASONS, WHICH ALSO INCLUDED THE NOVELLA RITA HAYWORTH AND THE SHAWSHANK REDEMPTION, OBVIOUSLY THE BASIS FOR THE OUTSTANDING 1994 FILM THE SHAWSHANK REDEMPTION.

It's Rob Reiner telling a classic Stephen King story. The result is an introspective and nostalgic look at the friendships we all had during our late-stage childhood years of wonder, adventure, and innocence. It was the time in our lives when every summer day seemed to last forever just as each school day unfortunately did too. Those were the friendships that taught us many of the lessons we would later use to help us succeed in the workplace. As Gordie so eloquently states at the end of the movie, "I never had any friends like I did when I was twelve. Jesus, does anyone?"

So, what can four brazen and adventurous, but innocent and naïve twelve-year-old boys teach us about today's workplace?

THERE REALLY ARE NO STUPID QUESTIONS.

During their journey, the boys spend a night sitting around a campfire in the woods, discussing the important topics of the day, such as what food you would eat if you could eat only one for the rest of your life. According to Vern, it's "cherry-flavored Pez . . . no question about it". They also discuss why the characters on the show *Wagon Train* never get anywhere. They just "keep on wagon training," Gordie says in frustration. Eventually, the conversation turns to deeper existentialism when Gordie asks, "Alright, alright. Mickey's a mouse, Donald's a duck, Pluto's a dog. What's Goofy?" Teddy replies that "Goofy is definitely a dog," to which Chris says, "He can't be a dog. He wears a hat and drives a car." At this point, Vern chimes in with "God. That's weird. What the hell is Goofy?"

On the surface, it seems that Goofy is a dog, and asking what he is would be the definition of a stupid question. But this is where we get our lesson. Sometimes, the question that appears to have the most obvious answer is actually the best one to ask. It's the one that prompts the largest discussion and can be the beginning of a robust brainstorm.

I think back to the first acronym I learned, "K.I.S.S." for "Keep it simple, stupid." I'm not even sure that they are allowed to use that in schools anymore, but it always stuck with me. Unless we are in a room full of Neil deGrasse Tysons, when we ask complex questions during a business meeting, they often go unanswered, or worse yet, each person tries to top the other by answering with a consistent string of buzzwords that would make Lewis Carroll feel a tinge of envy. You know the person who says, "Let's table that while we drill down into these bowling pins and see if we can move the needle with limited bandwidth. But, for now, let's take it offline, because I need a bio break, so make sure to put a pin in it and ping me later." Everyone nods in agreement, and you are onto the next topic without actually answering the question.

"Stupid questions" may appear to have simple answers, but they also create an environment in which everyone can contribute and perhaps provide a better answer that the team needs to move forward. It lessens the impact of "Buzzword Bob," and when everyone contributes, you may actually discover that the simple answer isn't so simple. This may actually help you uncover the differentiator, messaging, positioning, or product that leads to the success of your team and your business. So . . . what the hell is Goofy, anyway?

GOALS ARE ACHIEVED BY EMBRACING INDIVIDUALITY OVER CONFORMITY.

"WE KNEW EXACTLY WHO WE WERE AND EXACTLY WHERE WE WERE GOING. IT WAS GRAND."
— Gordie

When Vern said to the others, "You guys wanna go see a dead body?" he set them on a course to achieve a goal that would change their lives forever. Innocence would be lost, and the challenges of the real world would present themselves.

Vern also created a situation in which four best friends would have an opportunity to really get to know each other as they faced multiple challenges throughout their quest. The challenges were vast and varied: the local criminal gang, led by Keifer Sutherland, on the same mission to find the body; some very hungry leeches, a train barreling down the tracks and trapping the boys on a bridge hundreds of feet above the ground, the accidental misfiring of a gun, multiple losses of confidence, and something all of us are familiar with from being in teams at work and with our families at home: infighting.

What they learned along the way was that the key to overcoming these challenges and reaching their goal was the differences between them rather than their similarities. Yes, they were all twelve years old; yes, they lived in the same small town (queue John Cougar Mellencamp); and yes, they all had a shared sense of adventure, but it was how very different they were from each other that got them to their destination.

Gordie is quiet, smallish, and a creative storyteller. Vern is heavyset, nervous, and very much a follower. Teddy has a quick wit and a quicker tongue but possesses an angry darkness buried inside him. Chris is the most complex, outwardly confident with leadership qualities but inwardly insecure due to his poverty-stricken and very dysfunctional family. He is highly intelligent but doesn't realize it. Ultimately, each found something in himself that helped the team conquer a specific challenge, showing the rest of the group their true individuality and strength. Because they embraced this individuality over conformity, the boys reached their goal and found success.

Healthy businesses and the teams within them embrace individuality. When employees are allowed, or better yet, encouraged to be "exactly who they are" as Gordie stated, it creates an environment in which everyone has a chance to thrive. That is when really great things happen.

One of the coolest examples I've seen of achieving a goal while embracing the individual was when a space probe landed on a comet for the first time. There were cameras in the control room, and as you would expect, everyone was cheering and crying. It was an incredible moment. What the camera revealed as it panned the room was not wonky rocket scientists with pocket protectors and thick bifocal glasses, but something like a crowd at an alternative rock show. Here was the incredibly diverse group of men and women, some with tattoos, others wearing hoodies, and a few with visible piercings who had just steered a hunk of super-high-tech metal through space and landed it on a comet. Yes, landed on a comet.

I'm guessing that most of us don't land things on space rocks for a living, even if we might sing "Space Age Love Song" by Flock of Seagulls from time to time. We and our teams do have goals to achieve. If you find that your team is achieving its goals, but the results are typically of the vanilla variety, not providing breakthrough solutions, leaving you consistently underwhelmed, try embracing the individuality of each team member. In the next strategy session, encourage everyone to shed their corporate skin, remove their work mask, and be exactly who they are. You might be surprised by the outcome. If nothing else, it will create an atmosphere of acceptance that will make everyone more comfortable with each other and themselves. And that, my friends, as Gordie would say, is "grand."

CHAPTER 9

Planes, Trains & Automobiles

"I DIDN'T INTRODUCE MYSELF. DEL GRIFFITH. AMERICAN LIGHT AND FIXTURE, SALES DIRECTOR, SHOWER CURTAIN RING DIVISION."
— Del Griffith, *Planes, Trains and Automobiles*

I T WAS NOVEMBER of 1987. I was embracing my final year of high school with an ill-advised fashion statement by wearing a "Who farted?" shirt that got me kicked out of Spanish class. This was followed by the dual release of stink bombs in the cafeteria that smelled like 600,000 rotten eggs, and this is not an exaggeration. The best part? You stepped on them, and they disintegrated, leaving no evidence. I still want to meet the genius responsible for this invention. Yeah, it's probably a good thing that I'm not a parent.

With another pre-Internet holiday season approaching, the shopping malls were thriving, and the movie theaters were packed. Ushers were walking the aisles, flashlight in hand, shushing those who chose to talk during the movie. Today, we have theaters trying anything to get butts in seats. Full-service food and beverage, plush reclining love seats complete with blankets and slippers, rollercoasters, and trips to Mars. Okay, those last two aren't true . . . yet. And to think all they really need to do is bring ushers back and the people will come. Bank on it. Alas, that is a business lesson for another day and another book.

The box office was full of soon-to-be both generational and cult classics. Rabbits were having a tougher holiday season than their farm friend the turkey with an unenvious role in *Fatal Attraction*. *The Princess Bride* was ten weeks into its theatrical run and had officially immortalized Andre the Giant in the annals of pop culture history. Steve Guttenberg, Ted Danson, and the owner of everyone's favorite mustache, Tom Selleck, were in their first week of eliciting "Oohs" and "Awws" with the premiere of *Three Men and a Baby*. And one of the most surprising box office hits in history, as well as one of the most iconic 80s' movies saw Patrick Swayze and Jennifer Grey lifting their way into movie history with *Dirty Dancing*.

Not-so-fun Fact:

MY SENIOR PROM THEME SONG WAS "(I'VE HAD) THE TIME OF MY LIFE," THE HIT TRACK FROM DIRTY DANCING. UGH. I MUST CONFESS THAT I'M AS BIG A PATRICK SWAYZE FAN AS YOU WILL FIND. I LOVE ROADHOUSE, RED DAWN, THE OUTSIDERS, AND POINT BREAK, BUT THAT SONG OVER AND OVER AND OVER AGAIN FROM THE PROM DJ? AWFUL... JUST REALLY, REALLY AWFUL.

The Top 40 music charts were again delivering their insane mix of timeless talent and what can be called "Talent for the time." On the timeless talent side of things, there was Sting with "We'll Be Together," R.E.M with "The One I Love," Springsteen's "Brilliant Disguise," George Michael's "Faith," and Billy Idol's "Mony Mony." In the other category, we had Pretty Poison -- not to be confused with the metal rockers Poison, although they were there, too -- with "Catch Me, I'm Falling," Tiffany with "I Think We're Alone Now," and Debbie Gibson's "Shake Your Love." The latter two were discovered singing in a shopping mall in what was apparently the 80s' version of American Idol.

Television gave us to Johnny Depp's big break in *21 Jump Street*. As you might guess, I am not a fan of 80s reboots, but kudos to Channing Tatum and Jonah Hill for creating comedy gold with this one. *Full House* debuted with Bob Saget playing corny and cheesy perfectly, just like he did as the host of *America's Funniest Home Videos*. Watch his stand-up if you really want to see how very, very different he is from the characters he played. Lisa Bonet began charming all of us in the premiere of *A Different World*. This was also when we said goodbye to Ricky Schroder and *Silver Spoons*. We "pitied the fool" when Mr. T and *A-Team* got the axe. And we went down to *Fraggle Rock* for the last time. And for those who like gritty cop dramas, the cops of the groundbreaking series *Hill Street Blues* chased down their last criminal.

Planes, Trains and Automobiles, starring Steve Martin and John Candy and directed by John Hughes, hit theaters on November 25th, 1987. If the trailer was nothing more than those three names on the screen, this would have been enough to vault it straight to number one at the box office. That is some serious comedic genius right there, my friends. It's no surprise that with Hughes writing and directing it was another 80s masterpiece. It's the story of two men, polar opposites and complete strangers, Neal Page, played by Martin, and Del Griffith, played by Candy, who are thrust together through happenstance during the rush to travel home for the Thanksgiving holiday. Neal is a buttoned-up, very square, and uptight advertising executive. Del is a sloppy and slightly overbearing shower curtain-ring salesman with a complete lack of self-awareness. He has a big personality and a bigger heart made of pure gold.

The pair's three-day journey together begins with Del unwittingly "stealing" a cab from Neal after he has negotiated with and even paid someone else who claimed it at the same time. They don't actually meet at this point, but they do end up sitting next to each other on a plane to Chicago. Del proceeds to take off his shoes and exclaim, "Whoa! My dogs are barking." Due to a blizzard in Chicago, their plane is diverted to Wichita, where they struggle to find a vacancy in a hotel. Del manages to use his gift of gab with one of his shower curtain-ring customers who agrees to give the duo the last available room, a room with one bed.

From there, the fellows hitch a ride in the back of a pickup truck in the freezing cold which prompts Neal to ask, "What do you think the temperature is right now?" Del replies, "One." After thawing out, they hop a train that breaks down. Then they catch a bus, the tickets for which Del earns by selling his shower curtain rings as "stylish" earrings to girls they encounter at the bus station. That gets them only as far as St. Louis at which point Neal tries to strike out on his own by renting a car. This too turns into a complete debacle, prompting him to drop more "F" bombs in one scene than Eddie Murphy did throughout all of *48 Hours*.

Fun Fact:

EDIE MCCLURG, THE ACTRESS WHO PLAYS THE CAR RENTAL DESK AGENT UPON WHOM NEAL UNLEASHED HIS FLURRY OF CURSING ALSO PLAYED PRINCIPAL ED ROONEY'S ASSISTANT, GRACE ("HE MAKES YOU LOOK LIKE AN ASS IS WHAT HE DOES, ED") IN FERRIS BUELLER'S DAY OFF.

Furious, distraught, and without a rental car, Neal tries to get a cab to Chicago. He ends up on the losing end of a physical confrontation with the dispatcher and winds up back with Del who fared better with car rental. It's not long before said car catches on fire due to a careless cigarette toss by Del, which also destroys all the men's money and credit cards. The two eventually reach a train station via an appliance truck and separate once again only to come back together after a sympathetic turn by Neal. It's an incredibly heartfelt ending. For those who haven't seen it, I will not give it away. Just go watch it right away.

So, what did our uptight ad exec and our boorish salesman teach us about today's workplace?

YOUR CAREER WILL BE A JOURNEY. ENJOY THE RIDE.

"AS MUCH TROUBLE AS I'VE HAD ON THIS LITTLE JOURNEY, I'M SURE ONE DAY I'LL LOOK BACK ON IT AND LAUGH."
— Neal Page

Throughout the movie, our odd couple has a multitude of transportation challenges, but it is Neal who seems to consistently get the worst of it. Some of it is due to his pessimistic nature, which, at times, makes the lyrics from the 80s alt music groups The Smiths and Joy Division sound like a choir of cheerful birdsongs happily alerting the world to a new and beautiful sunrise. The rest can just be chalked up to really bad luck. In any case, the journey is tough for Neal both physically and mentally. When he's not being punched in the face or "picked up by his testicles," as Del eloquently states, or turning to ice in the back of pickup truck, he is thinking of his family and the fact that he's missing their Thanksgiving gathering due to his troubled journey.

It sounds like a career journey at times. Just when you think you've got it on cruise control, smooth sailing is ahead, or any number of bad clichés that every office has plastered on a wall somewhere, you find your career delayed, diverted, or catching on fire, and not in a good way. You've hit a rough spot. Maybe you've lost your passion. Maybe your passion has been ripped out from under you by a bad manager. In the words of the 80s pop rock band Loverboy, you find yourself "working for the weekend," which is no way to build a career.

There will be times when you feel unsettled or unsure about a particular position, company, or your professional journey ahead. It is in these moments that we can make our biggest career mistakes, typically by jumping at a new opportunity too quickly or for the wrong reasons. It happens; I've done it. It's likely that you will, too. And it's okay. When you reach that point, just heed the words of Mr. Miyagi, "Don't forget to breathe... very important."

Look, we aren't perfect. Anyone whose career journey is exactly as they dreamed it would be is, in the words of Madonna, a "Lucky Star." Your journey will probably look more like the chaotic but incredibly entertaining travels in *Bill and Ted's Excellent Adventure* than the substantially less bumpy traipses of *The Golden Girls*. This is a good thing. It's a journey, sometimes full of trouble and other times full of accomplishment.

So, get ready, because diversions, delays, cancellations, uncomfortable seating arrangements, and even explosions are all going to be part of your professional journey. It will be tough sometimes; no doubt about it, but here's the cool thing: they will all provide you with opportunities to learn. You will definitely "look back on it and laugh."

EVERY COMPANY NEEDS A GREAT SALESMAN

"I DIDN'T INTRODUCE MYSELF. DEL GRIFFITH. AMERICAN LIGHT AND FIXTURE, SALES DIRECTOR, SHOWER CURTAIN RING DIVISION."
— Del Griffith

Just thinking of John Candy's character Del Griffith brings a smile to my face. He was the definition of a great salesperson: affable, optimistic, and passionate about his product. More importantly, he is passionate about his customers. He knew how to close. He sold shower curtain rings as earrings for Pete's sake. He had the women try the shower curtain rings on and then delivered lines like, "I've got the deal of a lifetime for you," and, "These are the Diane Sawyer autographed versions." How about "This is Czechoslovakian ivory," describing the pure white ones, and "They are filled with helium so they're very light," when selling the clear rings; and perhaps my favorite, "This is an autographed Daryl Strawberry earring."

Unfortunately, not every salesperson is born with Del Griffith's gift of gab. If that had been the case, we would all have houses full of Chia pets, Ginsu knives, and Girl Scout cookies, though I do actually have a house full of their

S'mores cookies. Maybe they do have a little shower curtain-ring salesperson inside of them.

When we think of what makes a company great, we often talk about leadership, culture, vision, or brand. Of course, having a better product or service than your competitors certainly helps too. All of these things are very important, but success will come down to how well you sell what you do. For that, you will need your own Del Griffith. Maybe it's you. If you're the owner and founder of your company, then you know the hustle involved in building your business. Even if you are the very best at what you do, someone else very important, your first customer, needs to know that and believe it.

You might be saying, "But, Chris, you've been in marketing for over twenty years, and you are admitting that the key to a successful business is a great salesperson? Sales? Not marketing?" I know that the standard line is something about marketing and sales being like cats and dogs. Wait, this is a book about 80s pop culture, so a better analogy might be Tango and Cash, Riggs and Murtaugh, or better yet, Barbara and Oliver from *War of the Roses*. The reality is that a great salesperson can mask your company's other deficiencies while you figure out how to make the improvements and create the innovations necessary for the business to continue moving forward.

Besides the owner/founder/CEO, your salespeople are the face of the company. They are who your customers typically interact with first and most often, during good times and, more importantly, during bad times, when their relationship with a customer could mean saving a crucial account. Every company needs a great salesperson; someone who is affable, optimistic, and passionate about their product or service, and more importantly, their customers. Every company needs a Del Griffith. Let's be honest; every company has a Neal Page or two. Maybe your Del Griffith can make optimists out of some of them.

CHAPTER 10
John Bender and The Breakfast Club

"SCREWS FALL OUT ALL THE TIME.
THE WORLD IS AN IMPERFECT PLACE."
— John Bender, *The Breakfast Club*

I WAS A SOPHOMORE in high school when The Breakfast Club was released in 1985. As a typical 15-year-old, I struggled with the same adolescent issues and angst that have impacted generation after generation. I'm referring to the ones that John Hughes -- who was taken away from us way too soon -- director and writer of several movies discussed in this book and many others, including *Sixteen Candles*, *Pretty in*

Pink, and *Weird Science,* could so eloquently and precisely communicate through the teenage characters he created.

These characters and movies contained lines of dialogue that got us through high school and continue to provide us with business lessons and values even today. *The Breakfast Club* plot is simple. Five teenagers: "the athlete, the princess, the criminal, the basket case, and the brain" were all sentenced, for various reasons, to Saturday detention in the school library so they could "think about why you are here and to ponder the error of your ways," as Principal Vernon stated.

In a classic scene, John Bender, "The Criminal," played perfectly by Judd Nelson, removes the screws from the library door so it will shut and, thus protecting the group from Vernon's prying eyes. When the group is sternly asked by Principal Vernon about the door being closed, Bender says, "Screws fall out all the time. The world is an imperfect place." In Bender's quest to keep his antisocial and delinquent persona front and center for the group to see, he teaches us two valuable business lessons.

Fun Fact:

THE EGOCENTRIC ROBOT, BENDER, ON THE SCI-FI/COMEDY ANIMATED SERIES FUTURAMA IS NAMED AFTER JUDD NELSON'S CHARACTER IN THE BREAKFAST CLUB, THOUGH THEIR FULL NAMES ARE FAR FROM IDENTICAL. THE ROBOT'S FULL NAME IT "BENDER BENDING RODRIGUEZ."

THE BUSINESS WORLD IS IMPERFECT

Screws do fall out all the time. The business world is an imperfect place. And while some of these screws fall out due to circumstances beyond our control, others fall out because of how we react to the first missing screw. When things aren't going as expected with a specific team member on a project that you are leading, or just on a business day in general, try to remember that you do have the tools to fix the problem: patience, self-evaluation, determination, leadership, and confidence. We all have these qualities somewhere within us. It's up to us to apply them and put the screws back in the right places.

PROBLEM SOLVING

Real problem solving for the long-term requires initiative, creativity, and guts. Bender took the initiative to solve the problem of Vernon's annoying prying by finding a creative way to shut the detention hall door. By removing the screws, he made the challenge of getting the door open, and keeping it open, a much bigger one than just a doorstop could achieve. And it took guts, considering such tampering could, and ultimately did cost Bender a heap of future Saturdays in detention, but that was more due to his attitude. That may be the basis for a lesson in another book. The next time a screw falls out, just accept that the business world is an imperfect place, take a step back, and find a solution.

Afterword

I hope you enjoyed reading this book as much as I enjoyed writing it. Beyond the connections to the workplace today, the 80s were an amazing decade full of pop culture that will live on for generations to come. It clearly has a tremendous influence on popular content today. It wasn't just the movies. It was also the music, full of one-hit wonders, hall of famers, and a multitude of genres from synthpop to candy rock. It was the television, with the introduction of movie channels, MTV, and the beginning of shows like *The Simpsons*, still running today. It was the video gaming consoles like Atari and Nintendo taking over our living rooms while personal computers like the VIC 20 and Commodore 64 had every kid connecting to modems with their home phones, hoping to be the next Joshua from *WarGames*. Talking teddy bears, glowing worms, and kids from cabbage patches and garbage pails moved in on the traditional board games. Parachute pants, Members Only jackets, rat-tail haircuts, and pegged jeans were just some of the fashion faux pas to forget and remember. It was a magical time for creativity, invention, and, most importantly, the rise of the individual.

And, ultimately, we learned a very valuable lesson from The Breakfast Club when Andrew, the jock played by Emilio Estevez, said, "We're all pretty bizarre. Some of us are just better at hiding it, that's all."

Be bizarre. Normal is so . . . well, normal.

Bibliography

1. Breakfast Club. Dir. John Hughes. Perf. Anthony Michael Hall, Ally Sheedy, Molly Ringwald, Emilio Estevez, Judd Nelson. Universal Pictures, 1985.

2. Ferris Bueller's Day Off. Dir. John Hughes. Perf. Matthew Broderick, Alan Ruck, Mia Sara, Jennifer Grey, Jeffrey Jones. Paramount Pictures, 1986.

3. The Goonies. Dir. Richard Donner. Perf. Sean Astin, Josh Brolin, Jeff Cohen, Corey Feldman, Kerri Green, Martha Plimpton, Jonathan Ke Quan. Warner Bros., 1985.

4. Say Anything. Dir. Cameron Crowe. Perf. John Cusack, Ione Skye, John Mahoney. Twentieth Century Fox, 1989.

5. National Lampoon's Christmas Vacation. Dir. Jeremiah S. Chechik. Perf. Chevy Chase, Beverly D'Angelo, Juliette Lewis. Dist. Warner Bros., 1989.

6. Beverly Hills Cop. Dir. Martin Brest. Perf. Eddie Murphy, Judge Reinhold, John Ashton. Dist. Paramount Pictures, 1984.

7. Back to the Future. Dir. Robert Zemeckis. Perf. Michael J. Fox, Christopher Lloyd, Lea Thompson, Crispin Glover. Dist. Universal Pictures, 1985.

8. E.T. the Extra-Terrestrial. Dir. Steven Spielberg. Perf. Dee Wallace, Henry Thomas, Drew Barrymore, Peter Coyote. Dist. Universal Pictures, 1982.

9. Stand by Me. Dir. Rob Reiner. Perf. Wil Wheaton, River Phoenix, Corey Feldman, Jerry O'Connell, Keifer Sutherland. Dist. Columbia Pictures, 1986.

10. Planes, Trains and Automobiles. Dir. John Hughes. Perf. Steve Martin, John Candy, Laila Robins. Dist. Paramount Pictures, 1987.

Made in the USA
Lexington, KY
24 April 2019